Born of a Fox

Born of a Fox

Mystic Poetry of
the Divine Feminine by

hailey lynn

Copyright © 2022 hailey lynn (haileyhanson.com)

All rights reserved. No part of this book may be reproduced or used in any manner without written permission of the copyright owner except for the use of quotations in a book review or as visual art, with credit given to the author.

ISBN 9780578990842

Contents

Dedication

One | Poetry in Flesh   1
Two | Psychonaut Sadgirl   29
Three | Hurricane   63
Four | Scorpio Season   91
Five | Bitchy Bodhisattva   129

Photo   163
Index of poems 164

Dedication

With respect and gratitude to my beautiful mother
Vicki Lynn Hanson,

to my beloved grandmothers,

to all the women who have touched my life
and changed its course,
especially to Laura Segro,
who brought me back to life in Casa Sofia,

to Ayahuasca,

to pure confusion and chaos,

and to Kali Maa

hailey lynn

One |

Poetry in Flesh

*"Untroubled, scornful, outrageous - that is how wisdom
wants us to be:
she is a woman
and never loves anyone but a warrior."*
—Friedrich Nietzsche

hailey lynn

I surrender
to the space between my memories;
to the weight of the reflections
I can see clearly now
were of me.
I surrender
to the harshness of reality;
to the resistance I've been carrying;
deeper
than I can see.
I surrender
fully;
pulled by the currents,
exhaling.
I surrender
into emptiness;
everything
to nothing

hailey lynn

Straight out of space
bleeding through from another galaxy
She travelled thousands of years,
sifted through spacetime in fine grain,

Time sprung forth from the crown of her head
pouring down her being
washing her
in eternal emptiness,

Just to walk forward from primordial waters;
to step onto the shores of her ninth life

Dripping in jewels

Dipped in gold

Blessing the ground with each step of her soul

Her boundaries dissolved
and reformed, inside out

a living, breathing offering

an invitation
to the universe
within her

hailey lynn

These past few years have been nothing but unfolding

Everything that I've set out to do,
has only brought me to one cosmic initiation after the next

Rather than a path I've walked,
I've only watched life shred every bit
of who I thought I was set to be

I used to set goals, and then go achieve them
Now I set goals, and life shows me over and over
how the treasures are only within
and I have no control

Nothing has been consistent on this earthly plane
All the ground I've tried to stand on has dissolved
beneath my feet

I've cried more than I thought any person ever could,
and I've begged the stars for help,
in the most empty plea,
a few times

and I've surrendered
I've surrendered
I've surrendered to love, even where it wasn't
I've surrendered to love, even when I really knew better
…

hailey lynn

I've surrendered to death, several times
knowing deeply that its levity feels so much better
than to continue treading with the weight
of this earthly existence

Nobody becomes this surrendered on purpose
but no spirit becomes this strong on accident

hailey lynn

Beyond shadow work, I started falling into past lives
More like floating off into them though...
I can suddenly see and feel and know
these places and people and times

I become somebody I'm so familiar with

and as my memories surface,
bubbles of lost energies travel up my spine
I process others like a mushroom
their pain absorbed and transmuted by my biology
and I find so much compassion there;
so much acceptance for where I am and what's happened

hailey lynn

There are endless twists and tripwires,
the further you get from your center
and many people agree on the paths away from the self,
so they start to look real
until you ground in silence
until you run out of plans and reminiscence

There, you'll only find yourself
You'll only find your beating heart

hailey lynn

Can you tune into your subtle layers?
Can you feel the perception of your pure infancy?
Can you remember?

Don't let it taint you.
Though the world is poison,
it is medicine for the strong
the strong who've been initiated
through their own weakness
who've been birthed
over and over
through the shell of what they were

hailey lynn

Early-incarnation visions are coming through strongly
emerging from the shadows
that I'm comfortably looming in

I'm feeling like a ghost, everywhere I go
I can't tell if I'm really here, or lost
if everybody else can see my thoughts

Whatever this means, it feels potent
I can't hold onto it or let it go,

it just is,
and I'm in it now

A woman's beauty doesn't come from birth,
but from rebirth

hailey lynn

On the one hand,

my life feels like a series of sprints
in all the wrong directions
where whatever I'm running toward
eventually clubs me in the head,
and casts me back out into space

and I float for a while,
confused about everything

But on the other hand,

what else would I want for myself
than to wholeheartedly chase after all my temptations?
I want to go
I want to know
I want to see and be everything!

and even as I watch it always break me apart,
what is left behind each time
is more truth, shining through
less buttoned-up bullshit
more mess
more wonder

wider eyes than before

hailey lynn

It's all a game with myself
a crunch with my perspective
endless mirrors
a joke,
where the universe is laughing at me

a conversation between a thousand voices,
all pursuing motives that don't matter anymore

and the smoke is clearing now
more than I've witnessed yet in this lifetime

How didn't I see it before?

I'm only grateful

hailey lynn

It's beautiful to realize
as I take time to look back,
I can see how each rock bottom
was the next step on the path

Spirituality is not the death of your intelligence
or productivity,
it is the redirection of them,
away from the values that have been prescribed to you,
and toward the creation of your personal ideal world

hailey lynn

I stay true to my inner knowing,
even when I see myself failing
even in the midst of a mistake
because I am an expression,
a conduit

I am the truth, even when the truth is ugly.

hailey lynn

I learn through pain, typically
but I'm tired of crucifying myself

I expand by breaking,
but I'm sick of humiliation

Some of my experiences seem to just soak into my being
like I absorb the poison
instead of reacting to the medicine
instead of letting it cleanse me
I don't purge;
I conserve
and save up my energy
like inevitably there's a bigger fight coming

Every shaman I work with says the same thing to me:
You
are a Warrior

but I'm tired of fighting

I want to put my blinders on and
slip through the seems to liberation
I want to swim with less perception
to flow
...

hailey lynn

not take on every fight as my own
not extract every ounce of painful knowledge
from every little thing in my world

I want Nirvana

but I still want to know

hailey lynn

If you've never dropped out of society
for any period of time -
if there is no knocking in your soul
to be everything that you are, while you can -
if your heart's never cost you your entire life before -

then we probably won't have much to talk about

hailey lynn

To exist deeply within the eternal now;
this is the power of a woman

To be;
centered and serene

To magnetize the layers of eternity
into a single glance

hailey lynn

You don't need to sacrifice yourself again
You don't need to fight
You don't need to use your strength at all
because they'll beat you with strength every time
and even when you win, you'll still be losing

so lose

What is there to lose that hasn't already been lost?

hailey lynn

This woman is an ocean that will swallow you whole
A river
whose source you will never find
and whose rapids will tumble and break you apart

To give up on this type of woman
is to hide from yourself
to postpone the inevitable
because once you've drank from her,
no smaller pond will do
once you've been seen by her,
now two souls have been shown the truth

She is your reflection,
an amplification
the responder
the receiver
the truth
The Goddess
with the strength of the Gods

She will push you past your breaking point
She will test you by virtue of her soul

An awakened woman is a portal between worlds
and to love her with the depth of your being,
is to elevate yourself to Godliness
to become more than you were before
again and again

hailey lynn

I send my hopes out and they flow right back
I can feel the settling sands of time
how softened
how finished
how enough

I have done all I ever wanted to;
now I can simply be.

hailey lynn

My hips hold new perspectives;

Poetry lives all along my spine;

My shoulder blades keep secrets;

There is a paradise inside

hailey lynn

It's not for you
and it's not for me
It's for love
so it's for all
at once, and indefinitely

hailey lynn

True beauty is never expected

the spontaneous is all that is real

Only the raw,
the sharpest and the softest
is seen by the eye of the open
… is absorbed
… is illuminated

Not that which is hunted and harvested
not sought and salted and savored,
but seen.

hailey lynn

Looking into a small mirror
focusing
on the sharp little edges...
as if to look away is selfish
as if all else is me
as if I am God
when really,
God is everything
and I can see it humbly

hailey lynn

The moment you give up
is the moment you break through
just make sure the force you're yielding to
is no one else
but you

hailey lynn

You can't write poetry when you're afraid of being hurt

It is orgasmic
-- you must follow your bliss all the way
to the end of yourself

Whether you're speaking out your lonely truth,
casting away like the fool,
or handing your heart over one more time…

If you aren't risking breaking yourself apart completely,
then you aren't really writing poetry
then you aren't surrendering

Otherwise you're only pondering
and pondering has its place,

but anyone can ponder on the things they'll never do;

not everybody will become poetry in flesh

hailey lynn

Two

Psychonaut Sadgirl

*"What is the difference between a psychotic or LSD experience and a yogic, or a mystical? ...
The difference—to put it sharply—is equivalent simply to that between a diver who can swim and one who cannot."*
—Joseph Campbell

hailey lynn

I dive into deep waters by choice
not because I've lost my mind,
like a balloon out of grasp drifted into the sky,
but because I am already free;
nobody was ever holding onto the string

hailey lynn

He couldn't see me

So instead, he just kept on insisting
who I am

and to him, I was a child
incapable
had no life of my own
- that I didn't have a world outside of him.

I felt slowly, perceptively flattened by him
drained,
and then conquered
until I finally resigned to his idea that I was very small
and couldn't take care of myself;

and then
I didn't have the strength or confidence
to leave;

so I stayed
and in the meantime, I became nothing

in the meantime, I became nothing

hailey lynn

I hadn't been able to trust myself
mind and body
I felt tricked
misled
naïve and vulnerable

I only trusted the ground;
the gravity that could surely hold me – at least where I was

and so I flattened
softened
surrendered once again

hailey lynn

Invited me to see his van parked down along the beach
I said no thanks, and he asked, what about a palm reading?
He took my hand into his palms
and ran his thumb along a crease...
Looked up at me with smirking eyes,
and he said

You're naïve

hailey lynn

I'm not more beautiful for my brokenness,
but for the openness that the brokenness caused

hailey lynn

Sometimes I remember how it felt to be seven
and even the thoughts and dreams that I had then

I try so hard to teleport myself back there
close my eyes and imagine that if I open them,
I'll be right back there again
before I was tossed in a sea of expectations

hailey lynn

Will you help me?
can I get some more oxygen, please?
can you please help me smooth out these knots?
I can feel them full of sorrow
full of past

Should I be here or there?
and can I get some more now?
are these tears pouring out of me cleansing my soul?
or am I just strengthening the sad pathways?
and will you help me to figure it out?
if I breathe deep, and maybe less slouch?

I'm ready to stop carrying this all around,
but it's stuck in my head
like a song and a headache at once

Can I trade my addictions? can I start wanting less?
I'm already amazing at sitting and waiting,
but I've sat so long that I'm atrophying

When will I feel alive?
How can I trust anything after so many lies?

I don't want to be the martyr anymore
I don't want to glorify my ability to love
more than anyone else can give me...
…

hailey lynn

Clinging to my own glory is feeling like an echo chamber

it's this or it's that
it's good or it's bad
something in me is breaking
and I wish it would all fall apart and away already

hailey lynn

Love yourself because
the self that you've created/become
is random and neutral.
It deserves your love as much as any other self does;
As much as any other being

hailey lynn

They want to pierce straight through and conquer
to force surrender
to convince themselves they're powerful,
because they're able to take without really asking

and in their minds, they've done it
they've skipped right past the work

but then I'm left with the shrapnel
to pick up in my own time,
while they continue to explore

and now I've got a deeper wound than before

hailey lynn

Please stay the hell away from me
with your irresistible daddy vibes
while I'm trying to heal

hailey lynn

I only want the small nice things
the steam rolling from the espresso machine
the promise that later, I'll find the meaning
for the moment,
all else is invisible to me

hailey lynn

I speak, and I set myself free

I don't need to hold the power
of looming uncertainty

I don't need to steal reactions
from another's insecurities

I don't need anything
from you
to be me

hailey lynn

I can tell it to your face
or I can write it in a poem
either way, I know you'll hear it
but this way, I'll be gone

hailey lynn

I started developing a belief that I can't ever be happy
That even if I lived out all my dreams,
I still wouldn't be ok
I wouldn't be healed

I guess because I'd lived so many dreams before,
and I still found myself back at rock bottom
again and again

So I don't know what the answer is now

I guess just that I should love life at each moment;
When it's vast and fast and beautiful
and when it feels like my insides have spilled out
onto the floor,
and there's no point in trying to get up again

I guess I have started to feel differently about rock bottom
Since I've spent so much time there,
It's at least starting to feel like a solid starting point
… to something

I am glad that I can see that now

hailey lynn

Allow, allow, allow

Life might hurt us sometimes,
but we are clearing density toward levity
We are eliminating resistance
We are on our way to our personal idea of perfection

Keep picturing it,
and in the meantime
trust, trust, trust
allow, allow, allow

hailey lynn

Again the line between my dreams and reality
begins to blur
I recognize all my emotions and memories,
feeling more integrated into each of them at once,
as they come forward sporadically

and it feels so good
to live halfway in a world of my own abstract creation...
I feel I finally have the boundaries
to spread my love around again
to not be bombarded
with the harshness of others' assertions;
to make this world a better place

hailey lynn

Allow yourself to float off
to the place where everything makes perfect sense
the place where softness holds you
in clouds of
peaceful serenity
and become familiarized
with the fizzling elation

and then
come back to earth
and have a fresh look around at things

and then
dismantle
the shit
out of everything heavy
that's stuck in your way

hailey lynn

I don't want any other person
who sees themselves flying through the windy desert
who dreams of wild nature
who wants to live a crazy, quiet, wonderous life
of experimenting and wandering
and throwing themselves humbly
into the most foreign situations they can dream of...
who finds themselves lost in novels
and poetry
that teleport them to a far-off place they yearn to visit
a fire they wish to sit around
a train they want to catch
a tear they'd cry that no one else will ever see
I don't want one more of them to live a sad existence
I don't want one more of them to be strangled
by modern demands
I don't want one more of them to be depressed instead

hailey lynn

I don't really make promises to myself anymore...

Not because I don't trust myself
but because
If I'm centered enough to follow my inner knowing,
moment by moment,
then I know that all right things will get done anyway

The only promise worth making
is the one that can only be fulfilled right now

It is to be fully here;
Fully aware;
More fully expressed

hailey lynn

I didn't stop loving you
I stopped whittling myself down
to cooperate in a game
that made you feel like you could win at something

You didn't stop loving me;
You could never even see me.

hailey lynn

Less focus on the way things have been
more energy toward the way things are becoming

I'm manifesting the future either way, anyway

hailey lynn

Self-sabotage is a disguise your comfort zone wears.
It's a veil;
The trap that's laid over a cross-road,
so you won't even see that it's there

At the bottom of the trap,
is a warm, squishy embrace
… and you'll be happy for a minute;
until you wake back up and realize
that moving forward
now requires climbing out

hailey lynn

The efforts I've put into life,
over time,
have given me more and more space to lose my mind
and more and more benefits from doing so

hailey lynn

Ice cream scoop of consciousness
scraping the corners of
the carton of
my most melted
memories
coming out in
bits
and strips
of film
in flames
transformed
to steam;

fueling me

hailey lynn

I can feel the churning
the twisting and rising
the brief brushstrokes of insanity

I can see the flashes
the faces
the visions of who I might become

hailey lynn

I'm witnessing myself fall into the trance of America
the trance of unimaginative ease and convenience
The straight lines
that everybody fits into
and fights each other for space within

The time passes by faster here
days fly off into vortexes
and I duck for hiding here and there
Seeking space to exist where there is no monitoring

space to commune with spirit without suspicion

I hear the fear, not only in the taunting media
but painted with broad strokes
behind the words of the people
who believe they're speaking about the whole world

The signs
The phrases
The accepted common symbolism

It's like nobody ever asked why
…

hailey lynn

It almost feels like I'm not here
like I'm dead already,
or on another plane, in the same space
Always surrounded, but always alone

Is this my depression,
or their mass hypnosis?

Is this my weakness,
or their strength?

hailey lynn

I'm not so in love with my poetry anymore
I'm not so proud of the edges of my creative potential
I'm not so mad in confusion and love as I used to be

I had to work
to "build my inner masculine"
in his unreliability
in his absence
to survive in something other than self-destructive,
poetic love
which became nothing but a soul-level fistfight...
emotional abuse that was subtle enough to deny
on both sides;
but obviously felt

I had to learn to work with anger
to somehow escape the sadness
that could have consumed my entire life
To enter a dimension where I had control over something

because the trust I wagered was more than my own karma
what I gave was never coming back

At the bottom of the well, I started walking;
I never wanted to.

I'm almost backwards now
in a more peaceful, but less intricately beautiful place
and the gap between there and here
is still empty

hailey lynn

Sitting alone now
with my twisted perception
looking for the compromise
between connection
and deception

hailey lynn

To be disregarded is painful
but to love less -
not possible

Tobacco – for the anguish

hailey lynn

I stopped talking about it
I never stopped feeling it

Three |

Hurricane

"Hurricane Hailey. Leaving nothing but destruction in her wake, and people cursing her name. That is how everyone will remember you."

—A name not worth mentioning

hailey lynn

When you mistreat a woman,
she feels the force of your shadow
and transmutes your unconscious energy
into the embodiment
of your worst nightmare

hailey lynn

I feel like punching several people in the face

Instead
I'll sublimate

hailey lynn

You only hate me because I never backed down

Twist your reasons in a knot
Talk and talk me out of existence

The truth remains
and it's growing louder

hailey lynn

I can't be your circus act anymore

I can't keep on performing
for your friends
and for your ex
and for your fucking mom

I know you like to think you can hold down a wild girl,
but you can't;
baby bitch

not without a heavy dose
--you always loved me comatose.

Am I tame enough for you now?
Have I been domesticated?
I don't remember the last time that I was sober for a day
or the last time anyone heard what I really have to say

You say you like strong women,
but you can only handle me when I'm weak

You never wanted a real woman,
you just needed an accessory

Now that I'm drained of my life force and resources,
Oh! I see...
You can finally save me from something.

hailey lynn

What part of
"No."
"No, thank you."
"No gracias."
"La shukran."

"Get the fuck away from me."
"Don't touch me."
"Stop following me."
"Get off of me."
"I DON'T want that."

"I don't want to today."

"I don't want you to send me photos."

"I told you, I'm not into this."

"If you show up here one more time,
I'm calling the police."
"If you contact me one more time,
I'm filing a restraining order."

Did you mother fuckers not understand?

YOU'RE LOOKING WITH YOUR EYES AND
WITNESSING AN ANIMAL IN FIGHT-OR-FLIGHT.
NOT A GIRL WHO'S SO "TURNED ON" THAT HER
OWN WORDS DON'T MEAN ANYTHING.

hailey lynn

Oh you think women's empowerment is a cute notion?
Alright
Well that's fine,
go ahead and carry on with your life....

watch me walk away forever
and not even think twice

watch you lose your mind when you find
I'm not at home at night

watch me break your heart so bad
you accidentally
tell your wife

hailey lynn

I don't want to fuel your fires of absent compassion
I don't want to give you somebody convenient to blame

To move forward with judgement
is not to move forward at all

To point a finger at another
is to give yourself a name

hailey lynn

You are not my pillar,
you're an anchor

hailey lynn

The punishment
is that he's still himself
The revenge
is that I'm still myself

hailey lynn

Wild Woman Energy

It's why they're intrigued by me
and
it's how they get destroyed

hailey lynn

Oh I'm definitely insane
you can ask anyone that knows me
that girl who roams around alone and
never quite tells the whole story
Twisted
Mystic
in the mind and in the soul somehow
It's a mystery to which entity I might be bound now....

But I take this world straight to the face
and I nurture deeply
every space
I hold my sisters and my brothers
stepping lightly through their covers
I love
unconditionally
and I only talk shit artistically
I'm skilled in reversing time and gravity
Just like anybody who's been fucked
from mother earth
to sky daddy

hailey lynn

I never deserved anybody's violence
I never deserved to be pushed and thrown
I never deserved to be tackled
hit and held down
shot at
kidnapped
drugged
sedated
or raped
I never deserved to be dragged up a flight of stairs
I never deserved to be filmed against my will

I also never deserved to spend hours and hours of my life
explaining to *authorities*
why I "let" any of these things happen to me

Fuck the world that I lived in that told me I did.
It was never about me.

hailey lynn

I should've left
the first time I knew
I should've left

hailey lynn

I don't need to come after you
I don't need to try to "make things right"
or get even

When you look deeply enough in the mirror,
you'll see me there

hailey lynn

Trying to come around here like a wolf, still
but I've already shined my light on you

hailey lynn

Don't tell me that my anger is a masculine trait
rage is not the same as force;
it is a genuine expression

There is no goal to my energy
just because you're close enough to feel it

Do not project your shame onto me
because it's only the shame you feel toward yourself
over being afraid
of a feminine woman

hailey lynn

Please don't mistake me for your enemy

I am your reflection
on fire

"It's like you have so many rules for
how to interact with you!"
-he spit in my face

hailey lynn

He'd been screaming and puking for hours
flailing and hitting his face on the kitchen sink
broken glass covered the counter

we were all debating if it was time to call for help

He laid down on the floor
eyes nothing but black and white
and looked up at me,
purely
like I was an angel
a deity

like I was an answer

like I was his mother
and he
was reborn

hailey lynn

He could never break my heart;
only my spirit.

Because I no longer had the strength to leave.

hailey lynn

I do not tolerate in bed
not anymore
not for a second

Either we're cocreating magic
or my participation's ended

I no longer let anyone
masturbate using my body
as if I'm not here
because
I'm no longer anywhere else

I require your consciousness
because I've paid so dearly for my own
I'm not turning it off to turn you on
I'm not faking a flinch
and I'm not going numb

Come with me to the uncharted,
or you can't come.

hailey lynn

I'm done testing out my limits
I'm done hurting just for fun
I'll spend time with you if you make me feel safe
to unfold by myself
else,
get out of my universe

hailey lynn

I don't really know what to be grateful for today
I should be grateful for creature comforts
I should be grateful for people
I should be grateful to live more peacefully
than I have in the past...

But can I just be alone and ungrateful for a second?
Can I just be so fucking angry about the past?

It's not anger,
it's sadness combined with anxiety

hailey lynn

Even though I hate you,
I do hope your dreams come true;

Even though I've daydreamed awful things,
I hope none of them bloom...

Some part of me hung onto wishing
you could hurt as bad as me;
but truthfully,
I'm too at peace now
not to want you to be free

hailey lynn

Preferably, I would've gone mad a little more quietly

hailey lynn

Four |

Scorpio Season

*"The intellectual runs away, afraid of drowning;
the whole business of love is to drown in the sea."*

—Rumi

hailey lynn

I keep waking up before sunrise
I look out the window for the morning glow,
but it's not there yet...
But my dreams have been leaving me wide-eyed
and a little stunned
They keep showing me a mix of the men from my past
interchanging like they're all really one
Sometimes it's one split in two
and that makes sense to me...
the sweet side will walk me around the theater,
or the garden
and hold me by the waist like I might float away...
Often he'll whisk me away from the impassioned chasers,
neither of us even look back

I tend to wake up with the sweet ones though
sometimes I try to fall back asleep
to hear what they'll say to me
as if I'm not making it all up myself as I go

I used to lucid dream a lot, but not so much anymore
I watch like a movie now
and try to connect the dots after I'm awake...
I know I'm missing a man, but craving a God
So what's the point in reaching anyway?

hailey lynn

Thank you for your medicine;

Ouch.

hailey lynn

You burnt me,
but you set me on fire.

hailey lynn

Maybe I needed to be broken,
maybe that's where you came in
not to teach me any lessons,
but to uncover what was hidden within

hailey lynn

We were children for a moment
... don't think that I didn't notice

We were children for a moment
dipping our toes into divinity
swimming through the mental realms
and diving straight toward ecstasy

I wanted to give you more,
but something stopped me
I wanted to go deep,
but your shallows felt choppy

My shaky hope that you could open me
crumbled each time I regretted
how well I could see

...it looked pretty clear to me
that you had a need to feel powerful over something
and maybe I get off on feeling
powerless

Well if that was all you needed from me,
darling,

then here we'll sit.

hailey lynn

I gave you all my power
to see what you would do with it

Nevermind

hailey lynn

Is it hard to be with me,
an existential masochist;
to entangle with someone who is willing to be destroyed?

I like to give you the loaded gun
to see what you'll do with it
and in the meantime,
I want to see who you'll be as I destroy you too

hailey lynn

Anything
that
isn't
love
can
fuck
off.

hailey lynn

Love is everything
that love is not

hailey lynn

Am I leading you out of the dark
or just playing in it with you?

Maybe they are the same

hailey lynn

I prefer to remain hopeless;
It is my wish to be destroyed by you.

What else are we here for
than to break closer to God?

hailey lynn

Somewhere between
I can barely tolerate you
and
I absolutely can't resist you

I definitely want to die with you,
it's living with you that I have trouble with

hailey lynn

Every hour of the night, I let go.
In the morning when I woke,
I watched the switch flip back on;

Your love...
My insanity...
it had arrived again.

hailey lynn

Downloading
the memories
into my body

Windows in between dreams
of how it felt to be alive

I grasp;..
I go right back to sleep

hailey lynn

You should've loved me like the world was ending

You should've loved me like the war was raging
outside your door

You shouldn't gulped to drink me in
when you first tasted my skin
confident
you had the keys to open all of my doors

You should've fucked me like an unexplored galaxy

like you could make all my fantasies
and philosophies
come true

and the light behind my eyes
was the one thing that might
save you
because then
maybe it could have been true

hailey lynn

How many layers of myself can I starve out
before I'll be free?
How many addictions and subpersonalities
can I let bleed
out
before I'll be dry enough
to soak up something better?

hailey lynn

Somehow,
the more I love myself
the more I surrender to the force of you

hailey lynn

You woke up parts of me
that I thought didn't exist anymore

Yes, you did it through pain;
but to be seen
is all the same

hailey lynn

It's less painful for me to hate you

It's the love
that hurts the most

hailey lynn

I can feel that it's really over
I know now that I'm really done
now that I've cried even harder
than you ever made me cum

hailey lynn

I threw myself onto a plane
with heavy bags
full of our broken dishes
that cut me to pieces
when I finally unpacked them

hailey lynn

How should I act like things are normal?
How can I go about my day
when I can feel your energy still
rolling over me in waves?

hailey lynn

My entire victim complex
blown away

because I know I chose to love you,
but you still treated me the same

hailey lynn

Died again;
Turns out, you still don't love me

hailey lynn

What will happen?
Why am I always wondering?

Why am I reliving my whole life, and all my past lives?

This feels divine
This feels beyond anything I've ever experienced

hailey lynn

I used to like being alone,
enjoying my solitude

but now I only feel
the aching absence
of you

hailey lynn

Well I guess I'll just keep living in my fantasy
where your betrayal and your lies
were somehow meant to be

Where I keep broadening the picture,
holding space for your apologies

Holding you
while I'm here,
empty

hailey lynn

Your name
falls from my lips
effortless

My voice -
I've never heard it like this

I see you
committed
in the shape of my hips

I feel you
Divine witness
of my innocence

hailey lynn

No more words; only gravity.

hailey lynn

Let me be undomesticated

Don't torture me with anything other
than playing around naked

hailey lynn

Drunk on the taste of your breath
Mesmerized by the textures of your depth
Entranced in your rhythms
Dancing to my blissful death

hailey lynn

I'm lost, but I'm not giving up
I'm just dizzy from giving too much
When I'm sharp and not giving a fuck
I forgive myself;
I express what needs to be gone with the wind
I rewind
I rewrite the timeline

hailey lynn

I love me
for being able to see you
when nobody else seems to

hailey lynn

The morning sky glowed blue

another sleepless night
and headache full of
"how could you?"

hailey lynn

As much as I care for you,
I really cannot deny
that on the battlefield of love,
you always left me there to die

hailey lynn

hailey lynn

Five

Bitchy Bodhisattva

"One does not become enlightened by imagining figures of light, but by making the darkness conscious"

—Carl Jung

hailey lynn

May you be happy and free
and stay the fuck away from me

hailey lynn

Fellow children of earth,
You're not "being the light"
if you're pointing at another's darkness
You're not spreading love
if you think you're in a grand war against hate
Your growth is false
if it's over top of others
Your power is empty
if it's derived from anybody else

There are no others
The war is in your mind
There is only Now
There is only I
There is only Love

hailey lynn

Love is a frequency,
not a commodity
It cannot be given or taken;
only embodied,
and its manifestations shared

hailey lynn

To live gracefully
and purposefully
is to dance in synergy
with Time

hailey lynn

I became a fool on purpose
when I realized
the well-worn path had no benefit to my soul;
when I realized
that practicality was nothing but projected fear.

I'm not walking off of cliffs
-my intuition wouldn't do that to me
but I am doing things that make no sense to anybody else
or even to me oftentimes,

but I feel that to be a fool is
to accept life for everything it truly is:
painful,
beautiful,
terrifying,
and shatteringly free

hailey lynn

I'll arrive at my death as nothing but ash
nothing kept inside
nothing left

hailey lynn

Your truth may fall on deaf ears;
Speak it anyway

Your words might shatter illusions and cause outrage;
Embody your wisdom anyway

hailey lynn

When you work through your own karma
you align with karma
and then naturally end up
doing karma's best work

hailey lynn

You cannot convince somebody,
or criticize them,
into growing or changing.

You can only hold space for them
where they are at,
while continuing to walk your own path.

You can only love them, while holding onto unwavering love for yourself.

This gives people space to grow
- the space that you're holding for yourself
and inviting them into

this
is truly taking another as yourself
this
is space-holding
this
is unconditional love

hailey lynn

I've become skilled in the art of breaking my own heart;
of taking chances on people
and being fully let down

It felt like it was going to kill me at first
I had those nights of screaming into my pillows
and thrashing around my bed all night...
having vivid nightmares all the time...

I've spent many, many months alone
just re-experiencing my life,
finally reacting
and letting go of all the things that happened...

Feeling;

and I have to remind myself often
that the heartbreak feeling
is breaking me open more and more...

and the more open I am,
the better I can feel.

Today I laid on the beach and experienced pure ecstasy
-this has been happening a lot lately
like my mind and my body have become part of the wind
and I fizzle away
and I'm left giggling
at the seriousness I had once perceived

hailey lynn

I don't avoid pain;
I ask it to open.

hailey lynn

This life has softened the fuck out of me
sometimes I wish I were still sharp
-and I guess in some ways, I'm quite jagged...

But I'm so much fucking softer than I used to be.

I melt into people and places sometimes
I'm so patient that I waste my time
I'm so open that I let the worst things in
and I just take it all
like the ocean

Maybe I'm only bigger than before.

hailey lynn

Sometimes, to do the thing
which sends an angry mob running after you,
is the exact thing
which sets you right with your own heart

hailey lynn

Sometimes the fastest way to progress forward
is to lose the path
To stray so far
that you get knocked into a redirection

Pain leads to clarity
and cultivates wisdom

The spiritual path is not about perfection
it's not about staying centered

it's about consciousness
and alignment with the energy of the universe

and sometimes we need pain to bring us to consciousness

sometimes we fall asleep
when the road is too straight and narrow

we need to forget
in order for the universe to make us remember

This is where we'll feel our connection;
our truth of oneness with All;

in the reminder

hailey lynn

The path toward enlightenment comes
in waves of humbling illuminations

The feeling of:
Damn;
I've got a long way to go

hailey lynn

I shed light in the daytime
but my shadow writes at night

hailey lynn

My inner knowing doesn't need to scream
My truth is solid
even while no other ears are ready to hear it

hailey lynn

To see is to realize eternity,
but to love is to realize mortality.

hailey lynn

We're all interacting here in this karmic web
bouncing off of each other
and changing each others' courses

giving and taking
hardening and softening

some people's gems are surrounded in pain;
they hurt
because they're potent

those give me a gift
while also leading me back to myself

hailey lynn

The amount of your energy you have yet to call back
to yourself
is the forcefield around you that pushes people away

Only once you've called your energy back into yourself,
can you access the ability to take other people as yourself
-to truly love them

Art is capacity for love

hailey lynn

Peace begins within;
within the heart
within the self
within the body
within the home

hailey lynn

If we can exist in the same stillness,
I'm with it

hailey lynn

Realize that no man can give you the answers;
no person
no book
nothing of this world

You step into your power
when you let the world serve you;
sit back
and stop searching;
stop pulling

hailey lynn

Ascension is inherently painful
by the time you're calling it that

The lessons don't quit coming
and they don't get easier either,
but the faith grows
and the direction becomes clearer

hailey lynn

A lot of people believe
that to *grow up* is to close your heart
and become more rigid
so that you can *handle* more

Ironically, I think to *grow* is just the opposite.

hailey lynn

Travel was my first real love
and Yoga, my second;
Both have unraveled and rewritten
who I thought I was before

Travel taught me how to build up my defenses
against the world
Yoga taught me how to soften my edges

Travel made me strong
Yoga made me powerful

hailey lynn

Stop trying to get back to the way you once were
that peak moment you've imagined,
where you were the most confident;
or felt the most beautiful;
or were the most prestigious in some way.

That person does. not. exist. anymore,
and neither does the world that they lived in.

That biological arrangement doesn't exist
That neurological configuration doesn't exist
You are still that,
plus infinitely more possibilities
branching and growing from
every single thing you've experienced since then;

Become now instead.

hailey lynn

Every person that triggers you
is calling you into a higher level
of self love
and unfuckwithableness

hailey lynn

Nothing can be lost but expectation
Nothing can be gained but validation

hailey lynn

I cannot tell you who I am,
but you will know the sound of my voice

hailey lynn

hailey lynn

hailey lynn

hailey lynn

Index of poems

One | Poetry in Flesh

Surrender
Straight out of Space
Unfolding
Past Lives
Twists and Tripwires
Scorpio Season
Early-incarnation Visions
A woman's beauty
Wider eyes
Crunch
Each rock bottom
Creation
I am the Truth
Pathei Mathos
We probably won't have much to talk about
A Glance
Lose
This woman is an ocean
Be
Paradise Inside
For love, not you
What is seen
Looking into a small mirror

hailey lynn

No one else but you
Poetry in Flesh

Two | Psychonaut Sadgirl

Out of grasp
In the meantime, I became nothing
The ground
Palm reader
Not more beautiful for my brokenness
Sea of expectations
Oxygenate
The self
Conquerors
Irresistible daddy vibes
Small nice things
Speak
Long gone
A solid starting point
Allow, allow, allow
In the blur
Manifestation
Intention
I don't really make promises to myself anymore
You could never even see me
Manifesting anyway
Self-sabotage
The benefits of losing your mind
Ice cream scoop of consciousness
Brushstrokes of insanity

hailey lynn

The trance of America
The gap; in his absence
Compromise
To be disregarded
Tobacco
I stopped talking about it

Three | Hurricane

I don't make the rules
Sublimation
Upswell
Circus Act (*a dedication*)
No thanks
Notes from a past life
Absent compassion
Anchor
Revenge
Wild Woman Energy
Oh I'm definitely insane
"authorities"
The first time
Stoicism in the mirror
Shining
Feminine rage
Your enemy
Rules
Daterapist Reborn (*another dedication*)
He could never
Since you fucking asked.

hailey lynn

I do not tolerate in bed
Get out of my universe
No gratitude today
It's not anger
At peace
Preferably

Four | Scorpio Season

Missing a man, craving a God
Gracias por tu medicina
On fire
Uncovered
We were children for a moment
Nevermind
Existential Masochist
Anything that isn't Love
Love paradox
Playing in the dark
Holy Fuck
Somewhere in between
I definitely want to die with you
Your love... My insanity...
Windows in between dreams
You should've loved me like the world was ending
Let bleed out
Somehow
Through pain
It's less painful for me to hate you
I've cried harder

hailey lynn

Broken dishes
Waves
I chose to love you
Died again;
Divine
The aching absence of you
Living in my empty fantasy
Your name
No more words
Let me be undomesticated
Drunk on the taste of your breath
Rewind
Nobody else seems to
Headaches
Denial

Five | Bitchy Bodhisattva

May you be happy and free
Fellow children of earth,
Love is a frequency
Synergistic Dance
The path of the fool
Nothing but ash
Embody
Karma's best work
Unconditional love
The art of breaking my own heart
Ask
Big soft

hailey lynn

The angry mob
In the reminder
Damn Paradox
Part-time Demonic Priestess
My inner knowing doesn't need to scream
Eternity, Mortality
Karmic web gems
Inside-out Aura
Art
Peace begins within
In the same stillness
Power of reception
Ascension is inherently painful
To grow up or to grow
My strength and power
Become now
Unfuckwithableness
Nothing lost, nothing gained
I cannot tell you

www.ingramcontent.com/pod-product-compliance
Lightning Source LLC
Chambersburg PA
CBHW072004290426
44109CB00018B/2126